A spider's web caught by the early morning sun
in the Manifold Valley

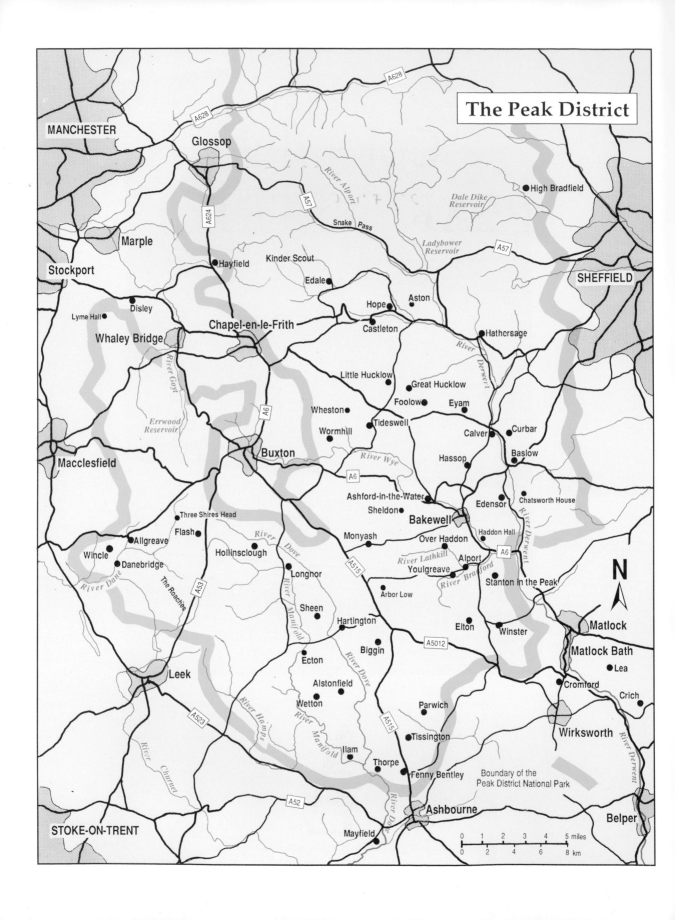

The Peak District

MANCHESTER

Glossop

High Bradfield

Dale Dike Reservoir

River Alport

A628

A57

Snake Pass

Ladybower Reservoir

A57

Marple

Kinder Scout

SHEFFIELD

Stockport

Hayfield

Edale

Hope

Aston

Disley

Castleton

Hathersage

Lyme Hall

Chapel-en-le-Frith

River Derwent

Whaley Bridge

Little Hucklow

Great Hucklow

River Goyt

Foolow

Eyam

Wheston

Curbar

Errwood Reservoir

A6

Tideswell

Calver

Wormhill

Hassop

Baslow

River Wye

Macclesfield

Buxton

A6

Ashford-in-the-Water

Edensor

Chatsworth House

Sheldon

Bakewell

River Derwent

Three Shires Head

Monyash

Over Haddon

Haddon Hall

A6

Flash

River Dove

River Lathkill

Alport

Allgreave

Hollinsclough

Youlgreave

Stanton in the Peak

Wincle

Longhor

River Bradford

N

Danebridge

A53

Arbor Low

Elton

Matlock

River Dane

Sheen

Winster

The Roaches

Hartington

A5012

Matlock Bath

Leek

Biggin

Lea

Ecton

River Dove

Cromford

Crich

Alstonfield

A515

Wetton

Parwich

Wirksworth

A523

River Hamps

River Manifold

Tissington

River Derwent

Ilam

Thorpe

Boundary of the Peak District National Park

Fenny Bentley

River Churnet

A52

Ashbourne

Belper

STOKE-ON-TRENT

Mayfield

River Dove

0 1 2 3 4 5 miles
0   2   4   6   8 km

Colourful
PEAK DISTRICT

Lindsey Porter

ISBN 1 873775 18 0

Front cover: Chatsworth House in the autumn
Rear cover: Dovedale, looking towards the stepping stones

Published by Ashbourne Editions
Sprinkswood
Clifton
Ashbourne
Derbyshire DE6 2GL
England

Printed by Gutenberg Press Ltd, Malta

CONTENTS

Introduction

◆

The Peak District is well known for its variety of scenery. Its beautiful valleys (known as dales or cloughs) and open moorland areas are loved by many. Indeed some 22.5 million people visit the Peak every year, such is its popularity.

We are fortunate in having such a wide variety of scenery across the Peak. The high northern moors and lower moorland areas of the west and east fringes have a landscape which contrasts with that of the limestone area. Even here, there is a large difference between the limestone dales and the rolling plateau landscape with its neat fields, dry-stone walls and linear tree plantations on the site of old lead mine workings. It gives the photographer a wealth of opportunity. This book is a delightful evocation of the area, drawing on the picture collection of Lindsey Porter.

Some of the scenes are well known features of this beautiful landscape, often from a refreshingly new angle, while some will only be known to those who explore the region on foot. It represents the area in all seasons: from sunny summer days to those cold, snowy or blustery days of winter, when the east winds cutting across the moors or limestone plateau remind us that we do not know our countryside until it is seen in all its moods.

In 2001 the Peak District National Park celebrates its fiftieth birthday. Here is a celebration of that birthday and the foresight of an earlier generation that was determined to encourage the conservation of our heritage. Despite the pressures of a changing and demanding world, we have responded to the challenge and through these photographs the evidence may readily be seen. The knowledge that the Peak District is in safe hands in its National Park Authority is its best birthday present by far.

In this book the captions have been written so as to add interesting and useful information to the colour illustrations. We start in the south-east of the Peak and move to the west before dealing with the central plateau and finally the northern moors. Wherever possible we have made an orderly progression round each area or followed the river valleys. In chapter 2 for instance the River Dove is followed upstream towards its source and then the River Manifold from its confluence with the Dove.

We hope that this book will inspire its readers to explore some of the off-the-beaten track places in this delightful part of Britain, where even on a summer Bank Holiday you can get away from the crowds. Recommended further reading is *The Landmark Visitor's Guide to the Peak District* which is the most comprehensive guide available, while *The Peak District: Its Secrets and Curiosities* has a wealth of information for those who wish to discover more of its fascinating facets. Both books are by Lindsey Porter.

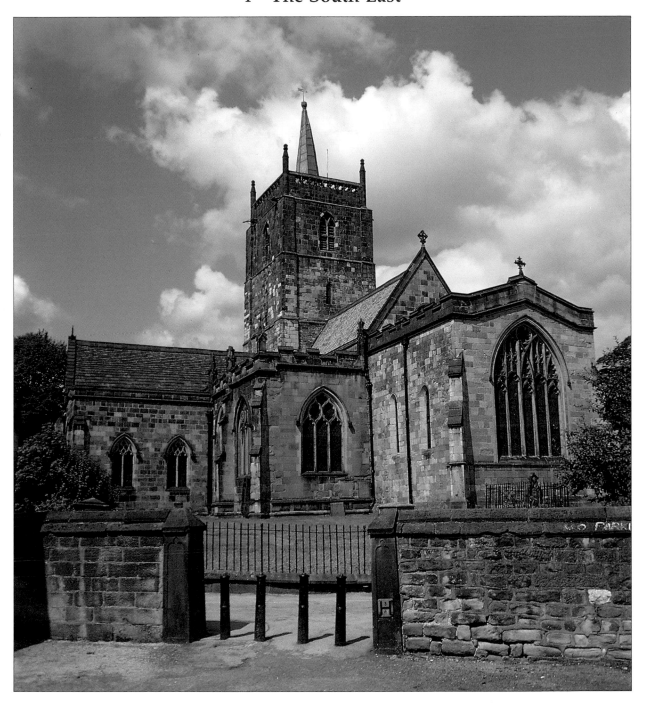

Wirksworth Church. This delightful thirteenth-century church is contained within a circular church-yard behind the main street. On the north wall of the church interior is a unique Anglo-Saxon stone slab carved with religious scenes. In the south transept is a Saxon carving of a leadminer, although this stone was brought to the church from Bonsall in 1870. Wirksworth has had a long connection with leadmining. In fact the oldest written reference to lead mining in the Peak District concerns the town and is dated AD835.

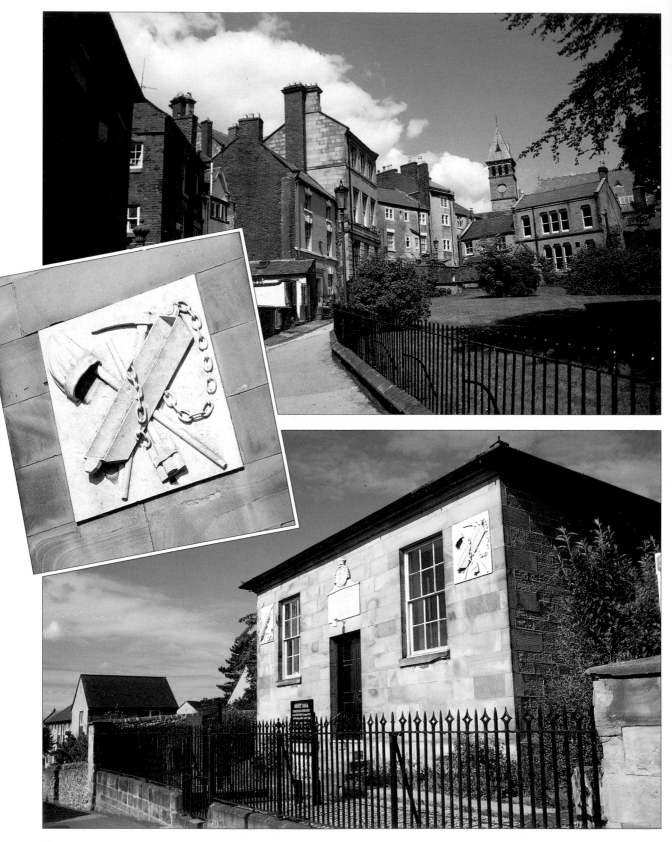

(*opposite upper*)   The circular path around Wirksworth Church is a fascinating back-water. Here are the houses at the rear of the main street. The building on the right-hand side is the Town Hall, built between 1871 and 1873. It formerly had a Butter Market on the ground floor.

(*opposite lower*)   Wirksworth Moot Hall erected in 1814 to replace an earlier building. Here is kept a bronze dish which dates from 1513, which was the standard measuring dish for the lead ore mined in the area. The leadminers' court still meets here. It is probably the oldest industrial court in Britain and the jury of twenty-four people still receive tobacco and a claypipe when the Bar-mote Court meets twice a year!

(*opposite centre*)   Detail of the carving on the Moot Hall, showing a lead ore measuring dish and various mining tools.

Cromford is a fascinating place to explore, with little passageways (gennells in local dialect) leading off the main street. One of these passageways leads to the Cromford Sough, a seventeenth-century lead-mine drainage level which still issues water into this catchpit. Behind these old cottages is the former village jail.

A mile or so south of Cromford Canal Wharf is High Peak Wharf where the canal met the Cromford and High Peak Railway. Nearby is the Leawood Pumphouse with a remarkable plunger pump worked by a beam engine. It is steam operated and has been restored by volunteers. Here can be seen the renovated engine below the huge beam. It is the largest surviving plunger pump in Britain.

Beyond Cromford is Crich, now the home of the National Tramway Museum. Here passengers are about to alight for a 3-mile round trip on a restored tram. The museum now has a total of about forty trams.

The Heights of Abraham at Matlock Bath are now much more accessible since the introduction of a cable car system, which gives a fantastic view of the River Derwent and High Tor. Here, ascending cars pause to enable passengers to admire the view.

The cars alight by the Victoria prospect tower, built in 1844. There are two show caverns on the site together with a restaurant and café.

Near Cromford is the lovely Lea Garden, with over 500 different species of rhododendron. Many species are now mature specimens on a sheltered terraced hillside garden. A visit here is always a delight when the flowers are in bloom.

Nestling under the plateau of Stanton Moor is the village of Stanton in the Peak. It is a small community of gritstone cottages, one of which is shown here, along with the Flying Childers pub, named after a racehorse belonging to the 2nd Duke of Devonshire.

On the east side of Stanton Moor is Earl Grey's Tower, built to commemorate the passing of The Reform Act in 1832. This compact area also has prehistoric stone circles, while there are fine views over the Derwent Valley.

Dating from the 17th century, Elton Hall has never been an important building. It differs from most villages in this respect.

(opposite upper)   The main street in Winster. The village grew as a lead mining community and has some interesting properties.

(opposite lower)   One of these is the Hall, shown here in springtime.

15

Middleton Top on the former Cromford High Peak Railway (now the High Peak Trail) line still retains its beam engine, which wound wagons up the adjacent incline. It is easy to find because of the chimney and is just off the Hopton-Cromford road.

(opposite upper)   Hognaston village, near Carsington Reservoir.

(opposite lower)   Carsington.

Tissington Hall, the home of the Fitzherbert family. The house is
Jacobean with eighteenth- and twentieth-century additions.

This is Hands Well, situated to the right of the hall, during the well dressing ceremony of 1989. A wooden frame is covered with clay and flower petals, leaves, mosses or seeds are then pressed into the clay. The designs usually have a religious or rural theme while this one even includes bars of music!

A detail of one of the panels from another of the village's five wells, showing how the beautiful effects are produced.

Preparing the well dressing frames.

(above) Here at Tissington the frames are seen soaking in the village pond. The increased moisture helps to prevent the clay from drying out.

(top right) Treading the clay at Tissington prior to applying to the frames. Salt is added to help keep the clay moist.

(right) Applying the petals to the clay is very time consuming. This creates the final design but has to be done quickly while the petals remain fresh.

2 Dovedale and the Manifold Valley

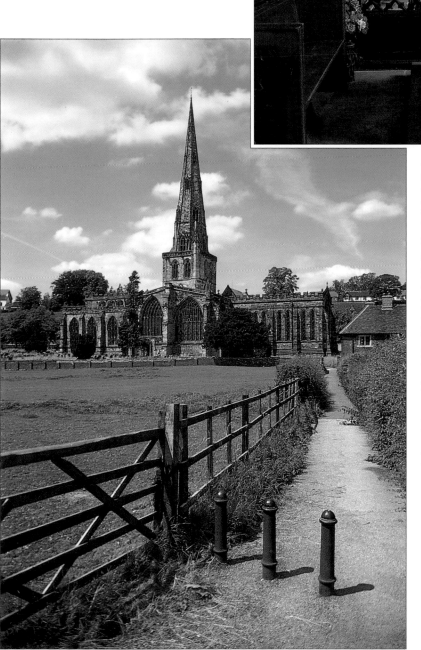

Ashbourne Church from the south. The church dates from the thirteenth century and still has a plaque giving details of the opening ceremony. It has an interesting group of early alabaster monuments, although it is best known for its nine-teenth-century carving of Penelope Boothby (*above*), a young girl whose death caused the breakdown of her parents' marriage and left her father a broken man. When the monu-ment had been completed it was exhibited at the Royal Academy and Queen Adelaide viewed it with tears in her eyes. Here it is shown in the church's north transept.

Ashbourne church with its spire rising to 212 feet. It is surmounted by a cockerel weathervane, a reminder of the Cokayne family crest. This may also be seen on the nearby former Grammar School in Church Street, dating from 1585.

This timber-framed property could be the oldest secular property in Ashbourne.
It dates from the late 15th century.

The southern entrance to Dovedale showing Thorpe Cloud to the right, which appears to be flat topped in this view, and the Izaak Walton Hotel in the centre.

The stepping stones across the River Dove at the foot of Thorpe Cloud.

(*right upper*)   Dovedale, just upstream of Ilam Rock.

(*right lower*)   Lion Head Rock, Dovedale. The ashwood here is of special importance, being one of the best surviving examples of the ancient woodlands which formerly covered the area prior to clearance by early settlers.

The entrance to Dovedale with Bunster to the left and Thorpe Cloud to the right.

Tissington Spires in Dovedale.

Four miles to the north of the former photograph is Mill Dale and this narrow packhorse bridge. It features in Charles Cotton's dialogue in *The Compleat Angler* of 1680 between Piscator and Viator. It is now known as Viator's Bridge.

The little shop at Mill Dale. The former mill here was a corn mill, later used for grinding iron ore to colour paint. This existed just upstream from the bridge.

(opposite upper) The Peak Park Joint Planning Board has restored several village pinfolds, where stray animals were once held until claimed by their owner. Biggin pinfold is one example. It is unusual in the Peak in being circular.

(opposite lower) Drystone walls without mortar are a feature of the Peak District. The area around Hartington also has several examples of this unusual type of stile. In the distance is the Tissington Trail. This stile may be seen on the A515 between Newhaven and Biggin.

At the end of the day. The setting sun highlights the pattern of drystone walls at Biggin.

The Tissington Trail north of Parsley Hay Wharf looking towards Cotesfield Farm. The Trail, once the railway line between Ashbourne and Buxton, is now a popular walking and cycle track.

(*opposite*) Hartington Hall, built in 1611, is now
a comfortable youth hostel. This and the nearby
Ilam Hall youth hostel serve the Dovedale area
and between them accommodate 50,000 visitors a
year. Both buildings have recently been refur-
bished at a total cost of nearly £400,000 and now
provide bedroom accommodation for families.

(*right*) Beresford Tower above the River Dove at
Beresford Dale. This prospect tower is all that
remains of Beresford Hall. It may be seen from
the river or better still, from the road to Wolfscote
Grange.

South of Beresford Dale the valley opens out into
Wolfscote Dale. Its beautiful scenery and easy
path make it a justifiably popular area for
walkers.

Hollinsclough, in the Upper Dove Valley, showing its distinctive village school, now replaced by a modern building at the rear.

The upper Dove near Hollinsclough with Chrome and Parkhouse Hills in the distance.

The market hall at Longnor

Hollinsclough Chapel

(*opposite*)   The Manifold Valley Visitor
Centre situated in the
former station.

(*above*)   The former turnpike road bridge at
Hulme End.

(*right*)   Ladybirds enjoying the summer sun
at Swainsley.

Wetton Mill in the Manifold Valley. It ground corn until about 150 years ago.

(*opposite upper*)   Thor's Cave from the road to Wetton. This and several other caves in the area have yielded prehistoric remains showing that they were used for shelter and burial purposes. There is a path to the cave from the river.

(*opposite lower*)   Looking towards the Manifold Valley from the Grindon to Wetton road. The wood in the distance is now a nature reserve.

The old 'Pepper Inn' at Back of Ecton. It is at the end of the road from Ecton.

Springtime in Wetton

This small reservoir called the Fish Pond collected water at East Ecton for a waterwheel on the 'front' or west side of the hill. It dates from the 18th century.

Ecton Mine from the Dale and the road from Warslow.

The Copper Mines at Ecton used to be the deepest and richest in Europe.
Now they are unused, dangerous and should be avoided. Here is the entrance to one of the later workings, driven in Victorian times at East Ecton. The stone work was necessary near the entrance to keep out soil and loose rock. Notice where the old tramway sleepers used to be.

Butterton Ford; one of only three fords in the Peak District.

(opposite upper)   The village pub in Butterton — The Black Lion — is now a popular venue for visitors.

(opposite lower left)   The church in Butterton, situated opposite the pub. The spire was an afterthought, added to an existing tower. A plaque in the chancel records an incredible act of bravery in 1844 when men tried to rescue others from a gas filled local mine. Each rescuer went in singlely and failed to return. A fourth man was restrained from entering the mine and a similar fate.

(opposite lower right)   This 'rindle' stone at Grindon records the ownership of an adjacent 'rindle' or watercourse. It dates from 1862, and locally the word is no longer in use.

(above)   Thorpe Cloud from Ilam where the Manifold joins the River Dove.

Sparrowlee Farm in the Hamps Valley

46

3   The Dane Valley and the Western Moors

Leek welcomes visitors approaching the south-western corner of the Peak District and makes a good base for exploring this area. Here is a winter view towards the town from Ballington Wood.

Gawsworth Hall, south-west of Macclesfield

Looking towards the Roaches from the ridge path above Back Forest near Gradbach.

Below the Hanging Stone on the path from Back Forest to Dane Bridge.

Horses on the same path. Between here and Back Forest, the path becomes a pronounced hollow way.

A contrast of seasons: beech trees in the autumn sunshine *(left)* on the lane between Swythamley and Danebridge, which gives views down into the Dane Valley *(below)* with a sprinkling of early snow.

(right upper)   The road from Danebridge leads to Wincle or Allgreave. The latter has some particularly fine scenery including this view towards Shutlingsloe.

(right lower)   Another approach to the valley is via Three Shires Head and this scene shows the view from the approach to Three Shires Head from Flash Bar. The buildings are at Readyleech Green.

Crag Hall, the country seat of Lord Derby, with Shutlingsloe in the background.

On the path from Dane Bridge to Gradbach

Jenkin Chapel, looking more secular than religious! It was built, as a stone informs us, in 1733 at John Slack's expense. The road is adjacent to what used to be an important saltway, a track used by pack horses to carry salt from Cheshire. It can be seen by taking the road from the Errwood reservoir (in the Goyt Valley) over Pym Chair and down the hillside in the general direction of Macclesfield.

(*opposite*)   The road from Jenkin Chapel nowadays runs southwards towards Wildboarclough. Near the latter is Cumberland Clough where a packhorse road headed up the valley and over the moor to the Cat and Fiddle Inn. At the eastern end of the clough, a cart track turns south, heading for Dane Bower Quarry. An embankment has been built across the valley at this point, causing this small waterfall.

(*right*)   The bridge at Quarnford near Gradbach with the road to the Roaches leading off to the left.

Although there is a parish of Quarnford, there is no village with this name. The only village in the parish — and the site of the church — is at Flash, which is shown here. Flash is the highest village in England, and is supposedly the origin of the term 'flash' money for counterfeits, but the inhabitants vigorously deny this!

The area around Flash is bleak, even in summer, and farming is a harder life than at lower altitudes. This view of Far Brook Farm and Turn Edge typifies these western moors.

To the north-west the Peak District lies close to the conurbation of Stockport and at Marple is the Peak Forest Canal. Here are two of the Marple flight of locks, lifting the canal towards Whaley Bridge.

(opposite)   The canal passes down through sixteen locks to the Marple Aqueduct where it spans the River Goyt. The aqueduct is 90ft high.

The Goyt Valley Trail and the Peak Forest Canal at Whaley Bridge.

4   The River Wye and the Central Plateau

Youlgreave Hall

Youlgreave church is well worth a visit. It has several ancient monuments (see across).

This chancel tomb chest is to Thomas Cokayne and dates from 1488.

Of a later date is this large monument of 1613 to Roger Rowe and his family.

A slow-worm in Lathkilldale. They curl up on the path when the sun is out. If found, please leave them undisturbed. Although looking like a snake, it is a legless lizard.

(opposite) Between Alport and Conksbury Bridge, the river is crossed by another packhorse way at Coalpit Bridge near to Raper Lodge. Here is the view upstream from this bridge. As the river rises on the limestone its waters are remarkably crystal clear and trout are readily seen swimming by. Even the waters of such famous trout rivers as the Dove, Wye and Derwent which all rise on gritstone or shale cannot compete for clarity. The bridge derives its name from coal brought by packhorse from the Chesterfield area.

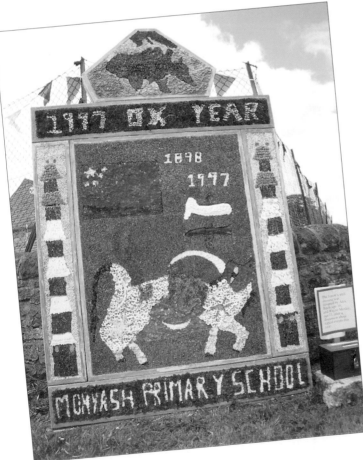

(above) Parts of Lathkilldale are in the Derbyshire Dales National Nature Reserve and special care must be exercised when walking though it. The reserve includes Britain's largest colony of the flowering plant known as Jacob's Ladder. The plants are fenced off but their significance is brought to the attention of visitors by information boards. The more people are aware of how sensitive the countryside is to change, the more likely they will look after it — a point seemingly not lost on English Nature.

(left) The childrens' flower arrangement for well dressing in Monyash. This was in 1997 — The Year of the Ox — which is represented in the design.

Dressing the wells.
Here a young helper lends a hand during petal laying at Tissington.

Owing to the porous nature of limestone, water drains in to it, taking minerals from the soil. This causes acidity in the soil which is conducive to heather and bilberry growth. Limestone heathland is uncommon, nonetheless, because of lime spreading by farmers. Here is a good bed of heather in bloom at Parsley Hay on the High Peak Trail.

Old lead mine tips are too laden with lead for most plants, enabling lead tolerant plants to grow. This is Spring Sandwort.

(right) Amid the fields to the south-west of Lathkilldale is the Arbor Low Stone Circle. The stones were originally vertical. The site may be visited and is off the Youlgreave to Parsley Hay road.

The vivid yellow of the flowering oil seed rape, which is now a common sight in Britain's countryside is also seen in parts of the Peak, as here near Parsley Hay. On the skyline to the right is the Bronze Age burial mound, or tumulus, known as Gib Hill. Unfortunately ploughing can destroy archaeological evidence undisturbed for centuries.

Monyash village green and its ancient cross shaft. The village, like so many on the limestone uplands, once depended on lead mining for its livelihood, but now agriculture — and tourism — are the main occupations

Monyash church viewed from across Fere Mere. Before the age of piped water supplies these ponds provided the only water supply. Monyash had four, but this is the only suvivor. In the central plateau there is little surface water and even most of the valleys are dry, their streams running underground in natural cavities or old mine workings,

One cannot travel far in this area without coming across some reminder of the ancient lead mining industry. Here is the Magpie Mine, between Monyash and Sheldon. This ruined building housed the huge beam engine which pumped water from below sough level. The scene is reminiscent of the engine houses which lie scattered throughout Cornwall.

Haddon Hall is regarded by many as the finest non-fortified
medieval manor house in Britain, with a fine collection of early
furniture and oak panelling, set in a glorious setting on the banks of
the River Wye. This view is from the old road to Coalpit Bridge.

(*opposite upper*)   Dorothy Vernon's bridge over the River Wye from
the hall garden.

(*opposite lower*)   The park seen through Haddon Hall's multi-paned
windows.

Haddon Hall: the lower Courtyard.

The Duke of Rutland created a huge bath (or swimming pool) in the basement of this property, Bath House, in Bakewell. It used a thermal spring for water, but Bakewell never became popular as a spa, being eclipsed by both Buxton and Matlock. The garden is now open to the public, off Rutland Square.

(opposite upper)   The Old House Museum at the rear of Bakewell Church has good displays of local history and industries, including early Arkwright textile machinery, as the town once had a small cotton mill.

(opposite lower)   A line of vintage tractors at Bakewell Show — perhaps the largest agricultural show in the Peak.

(above)   Sheepwash Bridge, Ashford-in-the-Water, probably the most photographed spot in the Peak District.

(right)   The village pump, Ashford-in-the-Water.

VIADUCT AND MONSAL TRAIL

(opposite) The classic view of the Midland Railway viaduct at Monsal Dale is from Monsal Head, although this picture is from a slightly different angle.

(above) The old railway line is now part of the Monsal Trail seen here above Litton Mill where it is crossed by the footpath from Brushfield. The trail crosses the viaduct before climbing up to Monsal Head.

(right) The viaduct was condemned by the nineteenth-century environmentalist John Ruskin as a gross violation of this beautiful dale when it was built in 1861. Today it has blended in with the landscape and it is difficult to imagine this well-known spot without the viaduct.

Below the Monsal Trail is Cressbrook Mill, originally built by Sir Richard Arkwright and replaced in 1815 by the present building. Arkwright's Apprentice House survives by the mill stream and is featured here with its Gothic-style turrets and windows.

The stocks at Wormhill. In the background is the memorial to James Brindley, the canal builder, who was born at Tunstead, nearby.

(below) Buxton Pavilion, built in 1871, established the town as a spa town in the Victorian era. It was extended four years later by this octagonal concert hall.

(right) Another relic of Victorian times is this letter box, to be found near the Opera House in Buxton and still in use.

The Classic-style parish church at Hassop. See also p85 for the view of the west front.

(opposite upper) The village pond in Foolow.

(opposite lower) Cressbrook Dale under a mantle of snow.

(opposite) The Eyre Arms, Hassop. Eyre was the family name of the Earls of Newburgh who owned Hassop Hall, now a high-class hotel and restaurant.

(right) The severe Classical Revival style church at Hassop, built for the Eyres in 1816-18. Charlotte Brontë used the family name for her novel Jane Eyre, which is set in the area around Hathersage.

Eyam Hall, built in 1672, with the village stocks in the foreground.

Eyam Hall is now open to the public. It has a craft centre in the former stable yard.

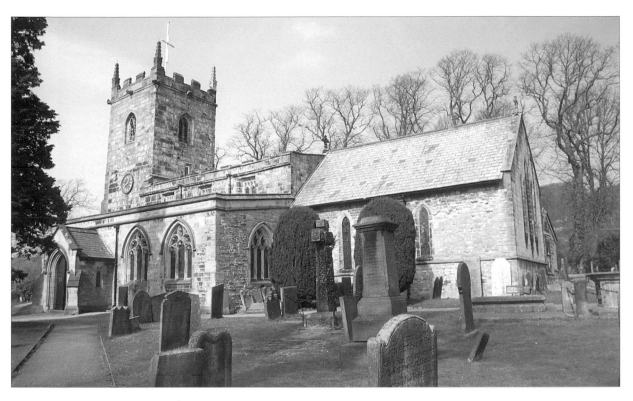

The lovely church at Eyam, with its memorials of the plague and its Celtic cross.

The George Hotel, Tideswell.

A rare sight these days, the replacement of traditional stone tiles (called shingles). This is at Bretton.

Also at Bretton is the popular Barrel Inn with its wonderful views. It is situated at 1250ft O.D. on Eyam Edge.

(opposite)   Two winter scenes in the Great Hucklow area, to the west of Eyam. The upper one shows Stanley Moor and the lower one, the view from Little Hucklow to Great Hucklow.

Waterfalls are rare in the Peak. This one however, shows a small stream falling into a collapsed swallet at Waterfall Farm, between Eyam and Foolow.

Peter's Stone from Wardlow Mires, between Foolow and Litton.

Little Hucklow

Adjacent to the Hope Cement Works is this worked out shale pit, now reclaimed for leisure purposes.

Peveril Castle at Castleton with its perimeter wall on the weakest side. To the right and behind the keep, there is a vertical drop.

5   The River Derwent and The Northern Moors

Horse trials at Chatsworth House. This magnificent palace, the home of the Duke and Duchess of Devonshire, with its gardens and park hosts a number of events in the summer, as well as welcoming those who come to see its treasures.

(above) The Orangery, Chatsworth

(opposite upper) The Chatsworth stables, built by Thomas Paine between 1758 and 1763 and now the refreshment rooms.

(opposite lower) Calton Lees, a little known hamlet on the Chatsworth Estate.

95

Chatsworth Mill, which was made ruinous in the severe gales of 1962 when a tree fell across it.

Edensor

Edensor village was rebuilt out of sight of Chatsworth House in a variety of styles. These houses are near the cattle grid into the village.

Queen Mary's Bower in Chatsworth Park, a reminder of when Mary,
Queen of Scots was a prisoner at Chatsworth.

A classic view of this lovely house from Paine's Bridge,
built in 1760-64 when the grounds were redesigned.

(above) The George Hotel, Hathersage

(opposite) A corner of Hathersage

(over the page, upper) Curbar Edge

(over the page, lower) Carlwark, near Millstone Edge, near Hathersage

This little bridge is usually submerged below Ladybower Reservoir. This photograph was taken from near to the site of Derwent church.

The Burbage Brook above Padley Gorge, close to where the Toad's
Mouth Rock is situated.

The millstone grit outcrops in the Curbar and Hathersage areas are littered with unfinished millstones and grindstones. This group, covered with bracken, is at Bole Hill Quarry where hundreds lie abandoned after the trade collapsed in the nineteenth century.

Fox House Inn which lies both within the Peak District National Park and the Sheffield City Boundaries. Despite its sign board showing a fox the inn is named after Mr Fox who built it. Tradition has it that Charlotte Brontë used this lonely inn as the setting for the place where Jane Eyre alighted from a coach on her flight to 'Morton' (Hathersage).

(opposite & above)   Millstones abandoned near Bole Hill Quarry, close to Millstone Edge.

Two views of some of the fine buildings to be found in the centre of Glossop

(right)   The crumbling face of
Mam Tor with the ridge beyond
extending to Lose Hill.

(below)   Beneath Mam Tor is
the Odin Mine where this lead
ore crushing circle survives.
Although it is a very ancient
mine which is mentioned in
records in medieval times it is
not quite as old as its Norse
name implies.

The ridge path from Mam Tor to Lose Hill with Back Tor in shadow in the distance. This path was an important packhorse route between Whaley Bridge and Sheffield via Hope and Yorkshire Bridge.

The Vale of Edale from Kinder Scout

(*opposite*) Edale from Hollins Cross on the ridge path from Mam Tor to Lose Hill. In the distance is Grindsbrook Clough.

Rushop Edge from Mam Tor.

The Old Nag's Head Hotel, Edale is a popular venue for ramblers.

Grindsbrook, the start of the Pennine Way

Edale village

Golden Clough and Ringing Roger, Kinder Scout

(opposite)   Kinder Downfall (on Kinder Scout) in dry weather. The ferocity of the wind often forces the water back over the top at times. To appreciate the scale of this view note the size of the figures at the top of the Downfall.

(below)   To the north of Kinder Downfall is this gritstone outcrop with the lovely name of Sandy Heys.

The top of Kinder Scout is covered in a thick deposit of peat with deep drainage channels called 'groughs'.

The moors were crossed by a medieval roadway between Hayfield and Edale. At its highest point is Edale Cross, now with a new surrounding wall, built by the National Trust. The Trust is engaged in considerable expenditure on conservation activity on the moors and welcomes donations to this worthwhile cause.

(opposite upper)   Bowden Bridge over the infant river Kinder. This old packhorse bridge is on the Hayfield to Edale road referred to in the previous caption.

(opposite lower)   Near Bowden Bridge is an old quarry, now a carpark. A plaque records that this was an assembly point for the 1932 Mass Trespass onto Kinder Scout which called for access to the moors — a freedom which we now enjoy.

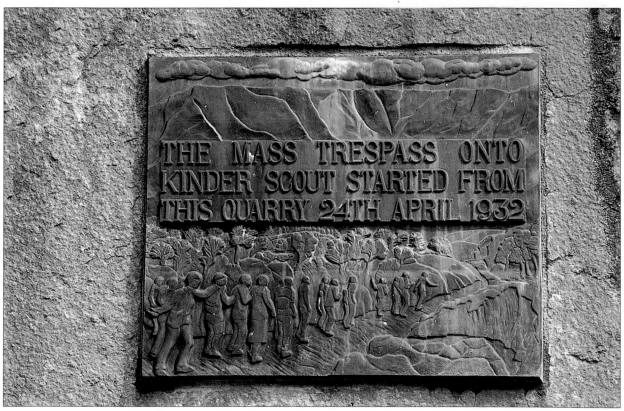

A further old road ran up William Clough, shown here, heading for the Snake Pass, or Lady Clough as it was known and the Woodlands Valley. It was the existence of these ancient roadways which proved that the closing of the moors by landowners was illegal.

(*opposite upper*)   A tributary of the Woodlands Valley is Alportdale. Above Alport Castles Farm is a landslip, known as The Tower, in view here on the skyline from the farm.

(*opposite lower*)   One of the barns at Alport Castles Farm is the setting for an annual 'Lovefeast'. The building is also one of a series of 'stone tents' and bunkhouse barns affording basic shelter in redundant farm buildings.

Rebuilding the stone wall along the Hayfield-Edale Cross to Edale
packhorse road, near to Coldwell Clough Farm. Mention has
already been made (page 118) of the work of the National Trust.
The Trust owns nearly 6,000 acres acquired under its Peak District
appeal and its High Peak Estate includes over 200 buildings and
miles of walls, some of which had been almost obliterated until
rebuilt, as here.

(right upper) Hayfield Church seen from the weir over the river.

(right) These two stones are guide posts on a medieval road south-west of Hayfield. They are known as Robin Hood's Picking Rods.

(opposite upper) Ladybower reservoir with its overflow channel exposed during a dry period. In exceptionally dry conditions, the water may drop sufficiently to expose the flooded remains of Derwent village. This has happened in 1959, 1976 and 1989.

(opposite lower) The Strines Inn, east of the Derwent Valley, overlooking the Loxley Valley and Boots Folly (see below).

(above) The watch house at High Bradfield Church, built to deter bodysnatchers.

Boots Folly, above the Loxley Valley and Strines reservoir. It was built to find work for unemployed men by a Mr Charles Boot.

Dale Dike Reservoir, the scene of Britain's greatest dam disaster when the dam wall collapsed in 1864 only 48 hours after it was completed. In the ensuing flood 238 people were drowned, fifteen bridges swept away and more than 600 buildings were destroyed or damaged.

Cottages in Holme village, north of Holme Moss.

INDEX

End of the day; The Mermaid Pool and The Roaches with
Bosley Cloud in the far distance.